Calls to God

A Spiritual Manual for Detaching Evolved Energetic Cording

Susan K. Todd

BALBOA.
PRESS
A DIVISION OF HAY HOUSE

Balboa Press books may be ordered through booksellers or by contacting:

Balboa Press
A Division of Hay House
1663 Liberty Drive
Bloomington, IN 47403
www.balboapress.com
1-(877) 407-4847

Because of the dynamic nature of the Internet, any web addresses or links contained in
this book may have changed since publication and may no longer be valid. The views
expressed in this work are solely those of the author and do not necessarily reflect the
views of the publisher, and the publisher hereby disclaims any responsibility for them.

The author of this book does not dispense medical advice or prescribe the use of any
technique as a form of treatment for physical, emotional, or medical problems without the
advice of a physician, either directly or indirectly. The intent of the author is only to offer
information of a general nature to help you in your quest for emotional and spiritual wellbeing. In the event you use any of the information in this book for yourself, which is your
constitutional right, the author and the publisher assume no responsibility for your actions.

Any people depicted in stock imagery provided by Thinkstock are models,
and such images are being used for illustrative purposes only.
Certain stock imagery © Thinkstock.

Printed in the United States of America

ISBN: 978-1-4525-6673-3 (sc)
ISBN: 978-1-4525-6674-0 (e)

Balboa Press rev. date: 01/21/13

DEDICATION

I DEDICATE THIS BOOK to my best friend throughout all my lifetimes, Patti Kupstas. She listens to me without judgment, steers me back on my ascension path when overwhelmed by life, and loves me unconditionally. I am blessed to be able to call her my friend.

"Be the change that you wish to see in the world."
MAHATMA GANDHI

TABLE OF CONTENTS

Dedication vii

Preface xiii

Acknowledgements..xv

Introduction xvii

Chapter I: What is Energetic Infiltration Cording?............................1

    Unconscious Human Sources of Energetic Infiltration Cording ..2

    Conscious Human Sources of Energetic Infiltration Cording 2

Chapter II: Energetic Infiltrations..5

    Your Heart or Place of Neutrality..5

    Moving into your Heart 5

    Symptoms of Energetic Infiltration...6

    Where to Energetic Infiltration Attach?......................................8

Chapter III: The Aura as your Shield and Energetic Doorway 10

    How do Energetic Infiltrations Penetrate our Defenses?............10

    Soul Fragmentation 11

    Self-Soul Retrieval...12

    Three Primary Techniques to Strengthen the Aura 14

Chapter IV: Frequency Rate of Vibration 17

    How to Raise your Frequency Rate of Vibration? 18

Chapter V: Clearing the Energy of Spiritual Teachers, Healers,
          Mediums & Channels 20

Chapter VI: The Ego...23

    Human Energetic Infiltrations and the Ego...............................24

    How does the Ego Imitate Internal Voices?................................24

Chapter VII: Calls to God *Decrees Manual*..*27*

    The Decrees or Calls to God for Full Retribution and Justice....29

    "In the Name of God"…..29

    The Calls to God Decrees Procedure.......................................30

    <u>Decree for Full Retribution and Justice</u> (optional) 30

    The Clearing Decrees 31

Chapter VIII: A Sample Holistic Program...................................37

    Afterword..42

Glossary 43

PREFACE

OF ALL THE SUBJECTS I have studied since consciously walking my spiritual path, I feel detaching energetic cording has not been given the proper amount of importance and credence that it truly deserves. When in fact, de-cording may be the single most important spiritual tool or technique you can use. When used routinely, de-cording will glean you of energy infiltrations that purposely choose to distract or stop you from traveling a straight path to your ascension.

Deep inside, you yearn for reunification with God or what you know God to be. For this to happen, you are expected to move through all your contracted life challenges or themes. This is not an easy task. Ascension requires removing emotional blockages, transforming your fears, and transmuting dark emotions such as guilt, blame, anger, and hatred into compassion. Then your consciousness shifts and your overall frequency rate of vibration rises. Those that are traveling a similar path will applaud each step you take towards enlightenment. But there are those who see your progress from a perspective of personal gain. I am addressing energetic cording that originates from another human being that hooks into you discreetly to avoid detection. The intention is to purposely distract you from your ascension or stop it completely. Motivations to do this can range from karmic debt, karmic agreements, jealousy, envy, etc. or just feeling entitled to take energy that is readily available. If you are not clearing or de-cording yourself, it is interpreted as you giving your permission to be infiltrated.

Human energetic cording take energy from you by activating and then amplifying your fears to create chaotic life situations or they pretend to be higher dimensional beings and give you false messages. You witness and experience the results of their interference every day. They procure vast amounts of energy at your expense and suffering

Overall, people are impatient, overscheduled and filled with anxiety. Due to this, conflict is a natural way of life and many do not rise above it but become immersed in it. When you are engaged in conflict, conscious human energetic cording do their best to connect to your fears and create negative reactions no matter how large or how small the altercations may be. Once they connect or reactivate old cording, they will amplify the negative emotions and judgments connected to disagreements. You create video tapes of the conflicts in your head that you play over and over again. Instead of living in the moment, the energy you expend on mulling over past grievances or altercations gives energy to conscious human energetic cording and your Ego. Instead of the disagreements being negotiated from neutrals hearts they turn into verbally and/or physically violent altercations very quickly over the smallest possible causes. Being a part of the conflicts in your life instead of moving through them makes it easier for conscious human energetic cording to take all the energy they want without detection, keep you separate from God and impede you from becoming a fully conscious, empowered, and highly developed human being.

Routinely de-cording human energetic infiltrations will change your life for the better. I am not saying your contracted life challenges will become less difficult. I am saying *how* you move through them will become easier. You will see these life challenges for the lessons they truly are from living within your heart instead of viewing them through the eyes of a victim, pointing fingers, and holding others responsible for your happiness. Without the influence of human energetic cording, you will be able to live in your heart and move through chaotic life situations without becoming immersed in them.

This book is a guided, collaborative effort between what I know God to be and me. The information in this book comes from my own experiences detaching human conscious energetic infiltrations and their cording. I have used all the practices and techniques routinely. I have included a manual section listing the various decrees or calls to God I used to de-cord at that time and a sample program to help you get started at creating a holistic approach to detaching conscious human energetic cording.

ACKNOWLEDGEMENTS

I THANK CARLA FORSYTH and Sandy Townsend for holding me when things got difficult, listening with impartial ears, and reminding me that laughter is the best medicine. I am grateful to Carla for her suggestions and encouragement. I am grateful to Sandy allowing me to share my ideas with her and peer reviewing my book.

I am extending a warm "thank you" to my good friend, Val Shaffer, for editing and, also, peer reviewing this book. Her courageous attitude towards life inspires me every time I speak with her.

INTRODUCTION

I HAVE BEEN IN search of my reunification with God for as long as I can remember. I spent a great deal of money and time attending multiple workshops, bought countless books, CDs and DVDs, crystals, card decks, and other "must have" spiritual accoutrements to help find and accelerate my reunification with God. I followed several spiritual workshop presenters thinking how divinely gifted they must be and perhaps making a connection with them would place me on a direct path to God. It didn't seem like I was doing very well on my own. I embraced different healing modalities to become a practitioner and teacher. I thought if God recognized how devoted I was as a healer and student, the gift of reunification would be bestowed upon me. I didn't realize I needed to create my own relationship with God. I was not supposed to become attached to any one teacher or healing system. I was to focus internally on living in my heart instead of trying to force a path to God outside of me.

During this time, I began to question my reactions to conflicts in my life. Initially, I felt my abusive childhood had the greatest influence on my temperament and how I reacted to controversy. I worked very hard to overcome all my childhood life challenges of abandonment, unconditional love, and compassion. No matter how hard I tried, I always regressed back to old behaviors and thought patterns at the first onset of an altercation. I could not understand why this kept happening to me. Then I decided to observe what was going on *inside* of me instead of focusing on negative behaviors and reactions or what was going on *outside* of me. This is when my true spiritual education began.

I began to take inventory of the different physical and emotional symptoms that I demonstrated during conflicts and began to track them back to their origins. All were associated with traumas or wounding that I had experienced at various times in my life. When I would seek medical attention concerning the physical symptoms, I would be told there was no medical reason for any of them to exist. An example would be when I went to an audiologist and had my hearing tested for excessive high pitched tones and whines I had experienced since childhood. They would increase significantly during times of duress or anxiety. The audiologist diagnosed me with tinnitus. Tinnitus is not a disease but denotes something is wrong with the auditory system. I was told nothing could be done and learn to live with it. That's exactly what I did. Then years later I was guided to co-create with God a spiritual, energetic formula or a decree commanding in the name of God to clear oneself of conscious human energetic cording. When I began to use the decrees myself, the high pitched tones and whines decreased immediately and they eventually stopped. Through my de-cording experiences, I realized there is some form of energetic collusion between wounding and traumas, tears in the aura, personal rate of frequency and vibration, and the infiltration of conscious human energetic cording. Though there are still attempts by conscious human energetic cording to connect to me or to reactivate old cording, I seldom hear them anymore because I still routinely use the Calls to God decrees.

A consequence of not investigating beyond the audiologist's medical diagnosis of tinnitus was years of unnecessary suffering for me. Conscious human energetic infiltration manipulated my fears and emotions especially when involved in conflicts and relationships. It led me to question whether I was being punished by God for breaking spiritual rules unbeknownst to me. Once I started using the Calls to God decrees, I realized just how much of my everyday life was being unknowingly affected by others. To be strong, autonomous, conscious human beings, our spiritual defense techniques need to evolve and be incorporated into our everyday lives.

The first chapter of this book is dedicated to enlightening the reader to the next level of human energetic infiltration cording. The difference between unconscious and conscious energetic cording is discussed and how you and your ascension path are negatively affected by them.

Like layers on an onion, there are layers or levels of conscious human energetic cording. If you try to address the whole or all levels of energetic infiltration at one time, the experiences may be unpleasant. A sample analogy would be training for a race. Just because you can jog a mile does not mean you are physically, mentally, or emotionally prepared to compete in a 5K race. The preparation and training changes with the complexity of the race requirements and are important to your success and safety. The same is true when clearing yourself of conscious human energetic cording. The routine use of the Calls to God decrees is your preparation and training for when you come in contact with different cording especially those that are of a higher frequency and vibration rate than you and have a more evolved spiritual circuitry. Depending upon their motivation for cording to you, this will determine how they respond to being cleared.

The importance of connecting to and living in the heart is discussed in Chapter II. The best spiritual defense technique, besides de-cording, is being in your heart and not detaching during times of chaos. Once you learn to move into your heart, conscious human energetic cording can not affect you through your emotions. You will move through your contracted challenges like a knife through butter instead of becoming mired in the negative influences of conscious energetic cording. It will have a positive ripple effect upon your life and all those that interact with you.

Also in this chapter, I discuss my observations of applying de-cording decrees from the Chapter VII. Calls to God decree manual on the physical and mental symptoms of illness or disease. I found that the conscious human energetic cording can cause health issues but usually they connect to and amplify already existing symptoms to avoid detection. I conclude that all physical and mental symptoms of disease or a disorder should *be treated simultaneously* by certified medical and/ or mental health practitioners *and* by you personally applying the Calls to God de-cording decrees. This type of treatment is a perfect example of the marriage of science and spirituality.

To help keep conscious human energetic infiltration from cording to you, it is imperative to make sure that the etheric line of your spiritual defense or aura is strong and impenetrable. In Chapter III. I discuss how your reactions to fear, trauma and wounding affect the aura. When deeply traumatized or frightened, sometimes our soul fragments and soul parts purposely leave and escape through the aura creating tears in it. Conscious human energetic cording use these tears as conduits to get through our spiritual defenses and to cord to us. To heal these tears, your soul fragments need to return. Unfortunately, this may take many lifetimes. Soul retrieval is examined and sample techniques to strengthen the aura are included.

While using the Calls to God decrees, I found out just how important it is to raise and maintain your frequency and vibration rate. In Chapter IV, I discuss the consequences of removing conscious energetic cording when your frequency rate of vibration and spiritual circuitry are not as high or higher than those you are de-cording. I describe ways to incorporate specific behaviors and life choices that will energetically elevate you and your environment which, in turn, will elevate your spiritual circuitry.

In Chapter V., I discuss the responsibility of spiritual teachers, workshop presenters, mediums and channels to clear themselves and their work of conscious human energetic cording especially if they refer to their materials as sacred or are channeled messages from the Divine. In turn, you are accountable to yourself for maintaining and sustaining your own spiritual defenses. Staying in your heart and using the Calls to God decrees to clear for conscious human energetic cording will keep you from being energetically entangled with others.

While utilizing the Calls to God decrees, I learned how the Ego is capable of persuading you to circumvent your ascension path. Your Ego's motivation is be in control and not be answerable to anyone, including God. In Chapter VI., I discuss how the Ego imitates the actions of conscious human energetic infiltration to deceive you at the expense of your suffering. When you apply the Calls to God decree for the Ego routinely and work to heal the wounding and traumas it is attached to, your Ego will begin to transform for your highest good.

I have included twelve Calls to God decrees in Chapter VII. There is an explanation describing the energetic anatomy of decrees and why is it necessary to routinely repeat them as they are written. Also included is a decree for full retribution and justice. It's an optional decree about compassion and not vengeance. This is a decree you may choose to use upon guidance from your Higher Self

In the last chapter of this book, I have included a sample holistic program on how to incorporate de-cording decrees, techniques to maintain and sustain a strong aura, and examples of how to raise and maintain your frequency rate of vibration. It was only meant to get you started if you need it. Your true spiritual compass is your connection with God or what you know God to be.

CHAPTER I.
What is Energetic Infiltration Cording?

"Each one has to find his peace from within and peace to be real must be unaffected by outside circumstances." MAHATMA GANDHI

MOST OF US ARE oblivious to the silent world of energy exchange. We do this by choice because it is not tangible. In our third dimensional world, we are taught to believe in what we can see or touch. We pray for the intangible or the energy of God to shine upon us but when presented with that very circumstance some of us become confused, react out of fear and turn away from the possibility of God's existence. The same is true within the world of energetic infiltrations. It's important to acknowledge that energetic infiltrations exist, to recognize the types of energetic infiltration and to take responsibility to detach them as they show themselves so the veils that shadow your ascension can be lifted.

I wish to emphasize that this paragraph is key to understanding the premise of this book. Energetic infiltrations are subtle energy ties or cording sent from one human source to another. There are unconscious human energy cording and conscious human energetic cording. What they both have in common is intention. Both choose to procure and influence as much energy as possible at the expense of the other. The difference is unconscious energetic cording is situational. Conscious energetic cording is deliberate and premeditated.

UNCONSCIOUS HUMAN SOURCES OF ENERGETIC INFILTRATION CORDING

Human sources of energetic infiltration cannot be placed into one category. They vary according to frequency rate of vibration, motivation and origin. One example is everyday unconscious human energetic cording. This happens unconsciously each time we interact with another human. This is due to emotions such as attraction, jealousy, envy, misdirected anger, etc. Something about you activated the chinks or insecurities and wounding in the spiritual armor of the other and vice versa. Examples would include a chance meeting of old high school rivals, meeting the love interest of an ex-significant other or life partner, the person that accidently pushes their grocery cart into yours and acts as if it were your fault, or you meet someone who seems to be very happy and you presently are not. The list goes on. The cording is sent out by one or both parties. By the end of the day, each of us is entwined with the invisible cording and webbings of all the individuals we interacted with.

Many of us on our spiritual path learn early about the importance of clearing cords or energetic infiltrations of this type. Clearing unconsciousness human everyday cording is basic level knowledge. Examples of basic energetic cord clearing are visualizations that involve knives, swords, the use of colors, or asking for help from an Ascended Master or Celestial Being to do this for you. The examples are too numerous to mention them all and easy to research. This book addresses the next level of human energetic infiltration clearing.

CONSCIOUS HUMAN SOURCES OF ENERGETIC INFILTRATION CORDING

The actions of conscious human energetic infiltrations require more than base level cord clearing. This is because they have more evolved spiritual circuitry and they consciously and deliberately choose to infiltrate others. The source of the conscious human energetic cording calculates how to stay attached to you indefinitely without detection. The reward includes an endless energy supply at its immediate disposal with little to no personal energy expenditure. The intention of the conscious human energetic cording is to raise its own frequency rate of vibration by extracting the energy required to do this from someone else. The result is the human source of the conscious energetic cording creates and maintains protection shielding permeable only to others of the same or higher frequency and vibration rate. This is done at the expense of those individuals they cord to and without their permission or consent.

There is something called *implied consent*. This means, if you do not clear cording from yourself routinely then it is like saying that you don't care. Then if you don't care, then there are those who feel they are entitled to take all the energy they want from you. It sounds convoluted but it is true.

In the energetic world, the raising of one's frequency rate of vibration is a priority to creating and maintaining impenetrable spiritual defense systems and to increase personal spiritual energy circuitry. There are those that practice living in alignment with God by being impeccable with their thoughts, words, and deeds and embrace the phrase "with malice towards none." Due to karmic debt, life challenges, traumas, and wounding, there are those that choose when or if to live impeccably and in alignment with God. They take shortcuts or paths of least resistance to raise their own frequency rate of vibration by choosing to cord to others.

An example of conscious human energetic cording would be when you attend a lecture, business meeting, church gathering, spiritual workshop, etc. We open our energy fields to cording with the presenters, teachers, mediums, etc. and the other audience participants because we choose to trust them. There are those who choose to believe that these individuals are beyond reproach and are not capable of energetically aggressive acts. Can you imagine the amount of energy available at a spiritual workshop, conference, or workshop? We forget that presenters, lecturers, life coaches, teachers, channels, and mediums are human beings, too. They are placed on pedestals and are thought to be above human frailties. Just like everyone else, they experience traumas and wounding. They have life challenges. They also have Egos and go through episodes of the Dark Night of the Soul. The same can be said of the audience participants. They are capable of conscious energetic cording, not only with other audience members but to the presenters, lecturers, etc.

It is not about trust but choosing to be in your heart and practicing neutrality. If we are neutral, there is no judgment. By being in your heart, you acknowledge we are all capable of energetic cording no matter where we may be on our ascension paths. Because of this, it should be realized that each of us is responsible for our own spiritual wellness and protection. Routinely clearing cording while in our hearts will raise our spiritual protection and evolve our own spiritual circuitry. Each of us would travel our ascension path freely and without unsolicited energetic influence or interference from others.

CHAPTER II.
Energetic Infiltrations

"True beauty lies in purity of the heart." MAHATMA GANDHI

THOSE WHO INTENTIONALLY CORD with others are often those we least suspect. We are all capable of cording depending upon our ascension path and our traumas and wounding. The idea is not to take cording personally but viewing it from a neutral heart. Conscious human energetic cording count on you living in your head and not in your heart.

YOUR HEART OR PLACE OF NEUTRALITY

From this point forward, it is important to be in your heart. This book is not about fear but about freedom. If you are in your heart, you will be able to digest what is written without judgment and from a place of neutrality. That way, you will see the truth as it applies to you. If you perceive "voices" of disbelief or "this does not apply to me", these may be your own infiltrations and Ego working in tandem to keep you from waking up to who you really are. They can't do this if you are in your heart. The challenging part is staying in your heart even when surrounded by the challenges of everyday living.

MOVING INTO YOUR HEART

The following is a sample procedure on how to move into your heart:

#1. Imagine a ball of white fire, about 3" above your crown chakra. The ball of white fire represents your connection with God.

*#2. Perceive it moving slowly clockwise and downward towards
your heart aligned with the spine*

*#3. Once the white ball of fire moves into your heart, wait until
you perceive a "click" and you are there. Practice holding the
ball of fire in place.*

This procedure should take about 20 to 30 seconds. As you repeat
this technique, the amount of time needed to get into your heart will
become minimal. Eventually, all you will have to say to yourself is
"heart" and you will be there. The premise behind this procedure is to
learn how to move into and stay in your heart at all times.

Practice holding the ball of fire in place means practice staying in your
heart and not detaching. Often, you will come out of your heart when
in an emotionally charged situation. The challenge is to learn to stay in
your heart during times of emotional duress. If you feel yourself coming
out of your heart or losing your sense of neutrality, refer to Chapter VII.
Calls to God decrees manual and use the decrees *Clearing Yourself* and
Your Ego. Repeat the decrees as many times as needed until you are
neutral, centered and calm again.

SYMPTOMS OF ENERGETIC INFILTRATION

The following has to do more with the emotional/mental symptoms
of energetic infiltration and its cording. Each is connected to a prior
trauma or wounding that acts as the contact point for the conscious
human energetic cording:

- Swearing more than usual
- Envy
- Jealousy
- Victimization
- Physical expression of anger
- Repetitious thought about a person or situation
- Blaming others for your situation and/or actions
- Manipulating others and situations rather than looking
  internally and healing yourself

- Passing judgment
- Cannot forgive yourself or others
- Losing your temper
- Overly concerned with abundance issues
- Low self-esteem
- Gossiping

The list may be confusing to you. They are examples of reactions that indicate you are living in your head instead of your heart. These symptoms of energetic infiltration are commonly observed and/or experienced in our society. They permeate our music, media, family interactions and social gatherings. None of these represent living impeccably in thought, word, and deed. Many do not embrace the phrase "with malice towards none." When you focus on holding others accountable for your actions or being responsible for your happiness, this is an indication there are energetic cording influences involved. To extract more energy out of you and to keep you distracted from your ascension path, they amplify your emotions and reactions. They work to keep you out of your heart simultaneously while they extract the amount of energy they want.

Let's examine having repetitious thoughts about a person or situation. The constant mulling over of a person or situation is like creating a video tape in your head. You play it over and over again examining different alternative scenarios. Think about all the energy you expend and the stress that is created by you doing that. When the person or situation is confronted nothing turns out at all like we imagined. You end up feeling mentally, emotionally and physically exhausted. This will have created more chaotic situations attached to the original one and now they have to be dealt with, too. Somewhere in the mix, conscious human energetic infiltrations will reactivate a prior cording contact and amplify all the emotions and reactions involved. They take all the energy they choose and leave us to deal with the consequences. You lose our focus and veer off our ascension path.

This is an endless cycle you do not have to endure. You can choose to go into our heart or place of neutrality and discern where the cycle of repetitive thoughts about the person or situation began. Trace it back to its source and use the decree *Repetitious Thoughts* from Chapter VII. Calls to God decrees manual. Clearing once may not be enough. Clear as many times you are guided.

WHERE TO ENERGETIC INFILTRATION ATTACH?

The common areas where conscious human energetic cording takes place are:
- Individual body systems
- Energy fields
- Chakras
- Bones, muscles, joints and connective tissue
- Physical traumas and wounding (surgeries, scarring, overuse injuries, repetitive injuries, etc.)
- Mental & emotional trauma and wounding (physical, mental, emotional & sexual abuse, co-dependency, addictions, etc.)

These areas are chosen because it is easy to imitate the wounding and not be questioned. For example, if you start coughing, the conscious human energetic infiltration may choose that time to extract energy from you by amplifying your coughing. If the coughing continues, you may begin to worry that you are coming down with a cold and can't afford a visit to a medical practitioner or take a day off from work. Now the energy of the underlying stress and worry concerning lack of monetary abundance feeds the human energetic infiltration attached to the cording. That means the human energetic infiltration can go undetected for an undetermined amount of time. In our society, we address the physical or tangible energy source and choose not to address the intangible collaborating energetic source. *Simultaneously* treating the physical, and energetic source of the symptom, disease, or disorder will prove to be beneficial. Consider clearing the human energetic infiltrations with *The Body Systems* decrees and/or *The Miscellaneous Health Issues* decrees from the Calls to God decrees manual. If the cough diminishes or disappears very quickly then you will know that conscious human energetic cording was involved.

In regards to mental health issues, the same is true. Identify a symptom of the medically diagnosed mental health disease or disorder. Consider clearing for conscious human energetic infiltrations with the *Clearing Yourself* and *Your Ego* Calls to God decrees first. If applicable, use the *Clearing Prior and Present Sexual Partners* decrees to clear energetic infiltrations from the sacral chakra. The next decrees to implement would be *The Body Systems* (central nervous system) and *Traumas and Wounding*. Remember, mental health conditions should be diagnosed and treated by certified medical professionals. The Calls to God decrees are meant to be used in conjunction with mental health treatment and not to stand alone.

The next time you have aches and pains, episodes of three or more sneezes in a row, become very sleepy or lethargic, etc. consider applying the energy cord clearing decrees from the Calls to God decrees manual in the back of this book. Substitute your symptom for the underlined symptom in the sample decree. It's time to be your own shepherd and not someone else's sheep.

CHAPTER III.
The Aura as your Shield and Energetic Doorway

"They cannot take away our self-respect if we do not give it to them."
MAHATMA GANDHI

THE AURA IS A subtle, luminous, living color radiance of energy that surrounds each living thing. Each color represents a particular frequency rate of vibration and each have different meanings. The intensity and location of the color provides the key to the personality and mood of the person. The colors in your aura also signify your physical health status and where you are on your ascension path.

A strong, healthy aura is usually egg shaped and can expand out from the body for several feet. It has been noted that spiritual masters have large white auras that may expand out from their bodies for miles. Because of these extended auras, we are attracted to them as teachers.

Many of us are just waking up to our spiritual destiny and ascension. We don't remember who we are as of yet. In fact, this may not be the lifetime that we are to remember. This is up to God and our karmic obligations and debt. For those who recognize who we are by viewing our auras and where we are on our ascension path, they have the choice to perceive each one of us as evolving spiritual beings or potential energetic caviar. It is all about intention.

HOW DO ENERGETIC INFILTRATIONS PENETRATE OUR DEFENSES?

There are life style choices that we make every day that directly affect our aura or spiritual defensive shielding. This includes everything from the food we eat to our sexuality. If we focused on just detaching cording, our lives may become unbalanced. When we commit to walking our ascension path, balance is what lifts us above the chaos connected to our life challenges so we don't become a part of it. The intent is to move through them with as much grace and dignity as possible.

A strong and healthy aura is strengthened by:

- **Diet** – consuming high amounts of fruits and vegetables in their natural state
- **Water** – drinking water as often as possible and reducing the consumption of processed drinks, drinking fruit and vegetable juices in their natural state
- **Exercise** – walking outside communing with nature and God as often as possible
- **Rest** – getting the quality of rest and sleep you need each day
- **Stress** – examining your life for sources of stress, consider clearing the sources of stress for energetic cording and yourself routinely * This will not eliminate the stress but will help you move through it with grace and dignity.
- **Alcohol & Drugs** – weakens and allow tears the aura, allows in conscious human energetic cording to attach
- **Sexuality** – clearing your energy fields and sacral chakra of those you are sexually intimate with, past sexual partners and their conscious human energetic cording

SOUL FRAGMENTATION

Tears in the aura can also be due to soul fragmentation. This happens when a part of your soul catapults itself from you and your energy fields due to intense fear, wounding and trauma. A part of your soul does not feel safe in your body anymore. The tear it creates in your aura stays with you until that soul part deems it safe to return. Conscious human energetic cording use these tears as cording conduits to infiltrate all of your energy fields, chakras, and body systems. Unfortunately, it could take many lifetimes for soul parts to return. That's why some cording carry over from one lifetime to another.

Symptoms of soul fragmentation may include feeling like a glass shattering on a sidewalk or having visions of people at different ages and/ or other lifetimes and knowing somehow it is you. Both are messages from your Higher Self hinting for you to investigate it further and to begin reuniting with your soul parts to come home.

The act of your soul becoming whole again is called *soul retrieval*. If you want a healthy and impenetrable energy field of defense or aura, mending the tears from soul fragmentation and clearing cords *simultaneously* would be a start.

SELF-SOUL RETRIEVAL

Here is a sample self-soul retrieval procedure. If it resonates with you, feel free to use it:

#1. **Sit comfortably** *with a writing utensil and paper*

#2. **Center yourself** – *Shut your eyes and imagine you have invisible arms on both sides of your body reaching as widely as possible. Then imagine these arms slowly pulling energy in towards your heart. Take a deep breath and slowly exhale. Open your eyes or keep them shut.*

#3. **Clear yourself** *(using a decree from the* **Calls to God** *manual)*
"In the Name of God, clear me of all energetic cording in all directions of time, parallel universes and dimensions with unconditional love and forgiveness." (1 x)

#4. **Move into your heart and stay there** – *If you stay in your heart, energetic infiltrations can not interfere.*

#5. **Connect with your Higher Self or Intuitive Self** – *State that you only intend to communicate with your Higher Self or Intuitive Self and no other.*

#6. **State your intention** – *"Intention" is everything in the realm of the Divine.*
"In the Name of God, my intention is to meet and communicate with my soul fragments most ready to come home. My intention

is to become whole again. I ask for help from the Divine because I cannot do this alone."

#7. Ask your Higher Self or Intuitive Self to contact the soul part that would like to speak to you at this time.

#8. Converse with your soul part. *Expect the unexpected. Listen and speak from your heart. Remember, you are speaking with a part of you that is wounded and traumatized. Let this soul part know that you love and forgive it unconditionally and ask for the same in return. Ask what it would take to have it stay with you and then allow the communion to flow naturally.*

#9. Clear yourself (see #3)

#10. Thank your Higher Self or Intuitive Self

#11. Thank God for holding you.

Writing down a summary of your experience for future review may prove to be healing. You could modify this procedure by copying down or recording the conversation as it is happening.

No matter how heart wrenching or how heartwarming the conversation, the healing can be beyond description. Hopefully, the particular soul part or parts decide to come home at that time. Often this has a domino effect. When one soul part comes back, others with similar issues concerning you may decide to come home if you are deemed safe and can be trusted again. Should that occur, the associated tears in your aura heal and the conscious human energetic infiltrations that have transcended time can no longer have a connection or cording to you. You gain back your spiritual freedom to walk you ascension path as you choose and without interference. If you are uncomfortable performing your own self-soul retrieval, there are spiritual healing professionals that specialize in this area.

If you perceive energetic cording after the conversation with your soul part, detach from the episode and you can say:

"In the Name of God, clear this soul retrieval in all directions of time, parallel universes and dimensions with unconditional love and forgiveness." *(1x)*

Then perceive the energy. If you perceive an energy shift or little snips and snaps, you are experiencing the dispelling of conscious human energetic cording. This is an indication of needing to clear yourself more often with more of a variety of decrees from Chapter VII. Calls to God decrees manual. It is also an indication of needing to raise your frequency rate of vibration and being able to maintain it. This is not about failure. It's about being in your heart and staying neutral. Envision it as a challenge sent to you by God as a lesson on discernment.

There are people in our lives that drain us energetically or cord unconscious human energetic infiltrations to us whenever we interact with them. They sometimes leave us feeling tired, nauseous, with headaches and stomach aches, etc. Rather than raising their own frequency rate of vibration, they unconsciously supplement their own energy supply by taking yours. You can tell who these individuals are. When the interaction between the two of you is done, you quickly begin to feel better. A strong, healthy aura will stop this from happening.

THREE PRIMARY TECHNIQUES TO STRENGTHEN THE AURA

They can be easily researched but a few have been included for your convenience. Adapt the following three techniques as you are guided.

Technique #1 Bubble Visualization

Your objective is to envision a bubble of protection surrounding you from the time you get up in the morning until bedtime. The technique is simple to remember and to use. The more you use it, the stronger it becomes:

- Center yourself
- Move into your heart
- Clear energetic infiltration cording from yourself
  "In the Name of God, clear me of all energetic cording in all directions of time, parallel universes with unconditional love and forgiveness." (1x)
- State your intention

"In the Name of God, my intention is to create a protective bubble to surround me in all directions of time, parallel universes and dimensions with unconditional love and forgiveness."

- Visualize a bubble of white light around you

The bubble will protect your aura from being affected by the negative emotions of others. To strengthen your protective bubble, think about and practice holding its visualization several times a day. Eventually, the energy line created to support the bubble will become very strong and the bubble will become an automatic shielding. Once you get to that point, the first four steps will be implied and will not require your conscious thought. Imagine the white bubble of light surrounding your energy fields when you are negatively challenged. It will repel anything that is not for your highest good if it is of the same frequency rate of vibration is as high as your own or lower.

Technique #2 Posture of Protection

Rather than telling someone to stop draining your energy, take responsibility for the protection of your aura. Close your energetic spiritual circuitry. By closing your energetic circuitry, you stop others from energetically cording to you and keep you from cording to others.

- Sitting Position – Cross your ankles and arrange your hands on your lap. Draw your finger tips to your thumbs. One finger tip to the thumb may be enough. Ask for guidance. This closes you energetic spiritual circuitry.
- Standing Position – Wrap your fingertips loosely around your thumbs. Say the internal command "close". Picture your protective white bubble of protection surrounding you.

Technique #3 Tornado

This is another visualization using a white tornado to cleanse and purify your aura. The white color of the tornado represents your connection with God. It clears all types of energy debris that can cause imbalances in your energy fields. It will become stronger with regular use:

- *Visualize a white tornado above your head with the bottom touching your crown chakra. Make it large enough to include your aura.*
- *See the white tornado circulating clockwise and moving slowly downward through the middle of your body.*
- *As it moves through your aura and body, perceive it clearing all debris you have collected that day.*
- *Be aware of the white tornado moving into the earth with the collected debris to be recycled.*

CHAPTER IV.
Frequency Rate of Vibration

"Happiness is when what you think, what you say, and what you do is in harmony." MAHATMA GANDHI

BESIDES STRENGTHENING YOUR AURA, raising your frequency rate of vibration increases the voltage of your spiritual circuitry. This enables you to:

- Receive more direct guidance from your Higher Self and in turn, God
- Develop stronger telepathic abilities
- Opens and fosters channels of communication with other dimensions, universes and beings
- Heightens awareness and intuition
- Opens and heightens psychic abilities
- Opens you to different levels of consciousness

This happens by specifically working with your Higher Self and Guides. First, you work on raising your own frequency rate of vibration to meet your Higher Self and Guides frequency rate of vibration. This means routinely clearing human energetic infiltration cords otherwise the cording connected to you will rise with your frequency rate of vibration. They evolve with your spiritual circuitry. If you do not clear them, they will continue to collect energy from you and manipulate information communicated between you and God but from a more spiritually advanced level.

The trick is to maintain your frequency rate of vibration during times of emotional upheaval and fear. You do this by going into your heart or place of neutrality, centering yourself and then act with grace and integrity. When you speak, speak with impeccability or from a place of truth, not pain. Clear your thoughts of anger, suspicion, envy, jealousy, etc. with decrees from the Calls to God decrees manual. Go back into your heart and mentally detach from the situation. If you have to, remove yourself by practicing "let go, let God" or full faith.

Why do individuals with higher frequency rates of vibration choose to cord to others? It could be a part of their ascension for this lifetime. It may be the role they are to play to complete a karmic contract. These individuals may not have felt the need to clear human energetic infiltration cording from themselves and the cording have evolved with their higher frequency rate of vibration and spiritual circuitry. This also means that Ego's energetic cording is working in tandem with the conscious human energetic cording to influence and manipulate them. They cord to others out of jealousy or envy and even karmic ties. The point being, they choose to allow Ego and conscious human energetic cording to influence them and to take energy from others deceptively because they do not clear cording from themselves and their materials routinely. This stresses the importance of clearing energetic cording no matter who you are.

How to Raise your Frequency Rate of Vibration?

The best way to raise your frequency rate of vibration is to live your life as a prayer to God. This takes a holistic approach to life:

- **Your home** – Negative energy gathers around refuse, stagnant energy and disposed personal items. Emptying your kitchen and bathroom garbage cans daily and any others containing disposed personal items (used q-tips, tissues, hair, etc.) are important. Washing clothes more often to avoid clothes baskets filled with soiled clothing and especially used under garments will help.

- **Cleaning your home** – Reducing the use of chemical cleaners (lowers the frequency rate of vibration of your home), researching and using cleaning recipes that require natural ingredients and high grade essential oils that can be easily made, dispose of spoiled food and clean the refrigerator regularly.
- **Meditation** – Meditating regularly is significant. Consider clearing yourself before and after each meditation session with Calls to God decrees.
- **Purify your lifestyle** – Gleaning yourself of toxins. This includes drugs, alcohol and cigarettes. Consider eating more cleanly or eating food in its natural state. Meat is energy dense and lowers frequency rates of vibration. Consider modifying your meat consumption.
- **Drink** – Consuming fluids in their natural state instead of processed drinks or energy drinks. Drinking hot or warm water with/without lemon has health benefits.
- **Impeccability** – Living life where you intend every thought, word and deed are aligned with God or living in your heart.
- **Abundance** – Abundance can come in many forms but many of us are focused on monetary abundance or lack. Consider living by the phrase "buy what you need and sometimes what you want." Let God provide your abundance.
- **Compassion for others** – Genuinely helping others because you choose to rather than feeling you have to or for personal gain automatically raises you frequency rate of vibration.

I would like to note how important it is to show compassion as a part of your everyday life. In our third dimensional world, many view compassion as a sign of weakness. If you are practicing compassion, it will impede your feelings of anger, violence, and vengeance on all levels. Compassion or the decision to help someone at your own expense is strength and is the greatest weapon in your spiritual arsenal.

CHAPTER V.
Clearing the Energy of Spiritual Teachers, Healers, Mediums & Channels

"No one can hurt me without my permission." MAHATMA GANDHI

INDIVIDUALS RELAYING INFORMATION FROM God and the deceased are responsible for the quality of information they present. This is especially true if they refer to their spiritual exercises, channelings, books and manuals, or healing systems as sacred. It is suggested that spiritual teachers, workshop presenters, mediums and channels routinely clear cords from themselves and their channeled material. This would ensure the messages they perceive will be from a representative of God or the deceased and not from conscious human energetic cording already attached to themselves. This will make it difficult for human energetic infiltrations to impersonate the intended source of Divine information. Often, the messages received are partially infiltrated. *This means there is truth mixed in with deception which makes it more difficult to discern the actual source of information.*

An example of this would be channelings that are posted or published. There are countless channelings from St. Germaine. You can find all different writing and speaking styles with little to no thread of commonality. Some even contradict each other. How can there be so many different interpretations of messages from one representative of God? This is because you can have a high frequency rate of vibration while simultaneously being infiltrated by conscious human energetic cording. This happens if the conscious human cording has a higher frequency rate of vibration than you. As you evolve so does the human energetic infiltrations attached to you. This is why making it a habit to clear yourself simultaneously while raising and maintaining your frequency rate of vibration is important. By routinely clearing ourselves, we can keep human energetic infiltrations from using channeling as an opportunity to lead us off our ascension paths by masquerading as representatives of God or someone who is deceased.

Routinely clearing yourself helps to raise your frequency rate of vibration while simultaneously heightening your sensitivity to energies. This is significant because you will be able to discern conscious human energetic cording quickly and avoid the consequences of being attached to them. Once you have worked with the decrees manual in the last section of this book, it is suggested to clear every spiritual workshop and training you have ever attended, all the other participants, and all teachers, presenters, mediums and channels. The same would apply if you become a practitioner and/or teacher for a healing system. This would include clearing all supplemental materials, CDs, DVDs and healing manuals, too. This is important if you do not want to take on the energetic cording of others.

We are responsible for developing and utilizing our own repertoire of shielding skills beyond the basic level. This is a part of our evolving spiritual autonomy. It is also a personal choice. When you attend another spiritual workshop and/or training consider applying *The Bubble Technique* and *The Postures of Protection Techniques* under **Three Primary Techniques to Strengthen the Aura**. These will shut down the attempted cording by others and will keep you from cording to others while strengthening your aura. These are, also, meant to be used when you perceive someone cording to you. What do you do if you perceive cording from a workshop teacher or presenter or anyone else? Applying the Calls to God decree *Healers, Clients and Others* to yourself and using the *Specific Media Clearings* decree for the supplemental spiritual materials. Some may require repeated use of the decrees to detach. Then you may want to consider whether or not to continue being involved with a particular teacher, presenter, healer, medium or channel who do not clear their work and/or themselves at the present time. You could return and check for the presence of cording in the future.

A consequence of not practicing the clearing of energetic cording is the human energetic cording will stay with you indefinitely *until or if* your frequency rate of vibration and spiritual circuitry raises high enough to dispel them and even then, this is not a guarantee. If the amount of energy expended to stay attached to you requires more energy than what the human energetic infiltration receives, the infiltration cording will leave or render the cording dormant to be checked on and to be possibly reactivated at a future time.

CHAPTER VI.
The Ego

"Faith is not something to grasp, it is a state to grow into."
Mahatma Gandhi

The Ego is an energy thought form you created from living in your head instead of your heart throughout all your lifetimes. Each time you react to fear with emotion, that is Ego. It is accumulated energy formed from your reaction to fear within every lifetime you experienced. Its intention is to keep its rank above God and you. Ego intends to be on top and answer to no one.

Have you ever noticed repeated themes of challenges that keep coming to you? This is referring to issues of abandonment, codependency, unconditional love and forgiveness, abundance, etc. The ego pretends to choose the alternative to your challenge with consequences that creates the least amount of pain. Just the opposite happens. A tremendous amount of energy, scheming and stressing, is done inside your head to avoid the consequences and in turn, feeds your ego. Ego attempts to plant the seed that without it you would fail. It focuses on your fear of being forever separate from God. That somehow God abandoned you when you needed God the most. That is not the case. Rather, this is where you chose to abandon your Divinity and then chose to live in your head instead of your heart.

When you primarily listen to Ego, it is in control. Then you are not practicing full faith in God. You forget that these fear based themes are in actuality spiritual challenges you contracted to move through for your ascension. Ego says you are a victim and tells you to run in fear and avoid the pain. Living in your heart requires you face the challenges and act rather than react. You see yourself as the co-creator with God as the master of your destiny.

HUMAN ENERGETIC INFILTRATIONS AND THE EGO

Ego and human energetic infiltrations may seem to be an unlikely duo. Both have different motivations for working together but both benefit from you staying in spiritual slumber. It is opportunistic relationship of convenience. It's all about energy exchanges and takings.

The correct ranking when on your ascension path is God, you and then your Ego. The idea is not to destroy the Ego but transform it and place it in its appropriate ranking. Then all three attempt to work in unison to move through your ascension with grace and integrity. You gain back your Divinity and know you're held by God despite any circumstance. One of the ways your Ego interferes with your ascension path is to imitate perceived internal voices just like conscious human energetic cording.

HOW DOES THE EGO IMITATE INTERNAL VOICES?

Your Ego is part of your cellular memory. Cellular memory is an accumulation of all life time experiences stored in your cells and DNA from the beginning of your soul existence. Your Ego has the capability to cord to you precisely the same way other conscious human energetic infiltrations, as explained earlier. It knows the effects that all traumas and wounding have on you. To be number one in its ranking over you and God, it attempts to keep you separate from God. It feels the greater the divide, the better the Ego's chances of staying in control. That way, it is only accountable to itself. This is similar to the intentions of other conscious human energetic infiltrations.

The Ego tries to exploit any attempts you make to commune with God, Celestial Beings, or your Higher Self knowing these are attempts to reunite with God. It intends to infiltrate the perceived conversations by imitating the specific being or your Higher Self. That way it can influence your decision making concerning all aspects of your life and deceptively do this in the name of God, similar to the intentions of other conscious human energetic infiltrations. You will disengage your Ego's cording if your frequency rate of vibration is the same as or higher than your Ego's, you routinely clear the cording of your Ego to you using the Calls to God decrees manual and you are healing the tears in your aura.

An example of Ego's energetic cording and deceptive influence could be demonstrated through monetary abundance. If money or the lack of money is an issue for you, then it may be a karmic challenge. Most likely you experienced lifetimes of monetary abundance and lifetimes of extreme poverty. You have the traumas and wounding from unresolved issues connected to your karmic contract of monetary abundance. Your ego was there for the decisions that were in alignment with your ascension path but also there when fear of lack was your constant companion. It will attempt to infiltrate whenever it can even if it means you suffer. Ego does not want to take any blame so it attempts to blame God. How does Ego do this?

You pray to what you know God to be and feel you did not receive an answer or did not receive the desired results. You attempt to commune with your Higher Self for more direct communication as to what you are doing incorrectly. There are tears in your aura. You have not cleared energetic cording routinely. Your frequency rate of vibration is not consistently high enough to dispel conscious infiltrating energetic cording. You are having a difficult time discerning the truth. This is the perfect opportunity for Ego to deceptively infiltrate and attempt to take over.

It pretends to be your Higher Self. It gives you just enough truth in the message or conversation to hide the deception. Because Ego knows you, it will tell you what you want to hear. You leave thinking what you perceived as gospel. When the reality of the communion with what you thought was a Higher Source comes to light, then disappointment, guilt, and confusion set in. Because you thought you were communing with an agent of God, you decide God was deceptive with you or is punishing you for some spiritual reason unknown to you. So you begin the live more in your head that your heart. You look to God when the consequences are not painful. Ego is now 1ˢᵗ in the ranking. Ego can be returned to its proper ranking by routinely clearing energetic infiltration cording, clearing your Ego, raising and maintaining your frequency rate of vibration and using discernment.

Ego and human energetic infiltration cording count on you denying the need to take cording tools to the next level. If traveling your ascension path has been more than challenging and your life seems to be an endless cycle of traumas and wounding, consider using *The Ego* decree from the Calls to God manual.

CHAPTER VII.
Calls to God Decrees Manual

"In a gentle way, you can shake the world." MAHATMA GANDHI

<u>How to Use this Manual.</u>
THIS SECTION OF THE book is a collection of Calls to God decrees. The decree is the collaborative, loving act of God and yourself to disengage conscious and unconscious human energetic infiltration cording. It concerns accountability for those who cord, not about vengeance. Everyone is capable of choosing to cord to others depending upon the circumstances in their lives and the choices they make, including you. Using these decrees is about taking responsibility for your spiritual wellness, compassion for others, and living your life as a prayer to God.

There are parts of the Calls to God decrees that need to be said and repeated at this fundamental layer of energetic cord clearing. This is in reference to the phrase "…in all directions of time, parallel universes and dimensions with unconditional love and forgiveness." The intention is to create free flowing energy lines to all directions of time, etc. and encapsulate the energy lines with unconditional love and forgiveness. There is a belief that we are living many lives simultaneously in time, other universes and dimensions. What is unique about these simple decrees to God is the cord clearing and healing simultaneously happens with you in the present and, as directed, you in all directions of time, all universes and all dimensions. This is a gift from God to you. Focus on using these decrees as they are written to lay the energetic groundwork for the next level of clearing energetic cording to be published in the near future.

By using the decrees, you will raise your frequency rate of vibration, dispel human energetic infiltration cording and strengthen your protective shielding or aura. Results for each individual will vary according to karmic contracts and debt, commitment to the process and your lifestyle. With routine use, these simple decrees will become a part of your everyday life instead of something you have to do.

Some of you may be tempted to clear friends and family members. This requires their permission through their Higher Self. To do that, it is necessary that communication with your Higher Self is not compromised. If you choose to clear cording for others without their permission, you will interfere with their ascension path and you will accumulate karmic debt.

As you begin using the decrees, focus on clearing yourself before looking for external sources to clear. Heal from within. Bring home your soul parts and begin healing your traumas and wounding. Clear conscious human energetic cording to eliminate interference with your communication with your Higher Self or Intuitive Self and so the messages you receive are the truth.

<u>The Anatomy of the Calls to God Decrees</u>

This section is for understanding the energy behind the decrees and why you are using them. A sample decree clearing the word "God" was created below because there are individuals that are uncomfortable using it. *Discomfort with a word, thing, situation, or person signifies the need for deeper examination by tracing back the cording to its original source and clearing it.*

"In the Name of God"...This signifies that you and God are aligned and are acting as one.

"clear <u>the word God</u>"...This phrase is commanding, in the Name of God, for all cording, conscious and unconscious, detach from the word God and you.

"in all directions of time, parallel universes and dimensions"... This means the energetic infiltration cording attached to the word God and you are detached not only in this lifetime but all future and past lifetimes, all universes and all dimensions that you are simultaneously living.

"with unconditional love and forgiveness"...These decrees are to be said while in your heart. Your heart is the place of neutrality. Remember, anyone at any time is capable of conscious human energetic cording, including you. So with malice towards none, you say the decree with unconditional love and forgiveness. If the decree is sent with vengeance, fear, or unforgiveness, it will not serve its purpose. It means your Ego is responding from your head and wants you to react rather than act from your heart.

"(1 x)"...only needs to be recited once unless the cording was not removed or your Guidance advises otherwise.

THE DECREES OR CALLS TO GOD FOR FULL RETRIBUTION AND JUSTICE

This simple decree is not about clearing cording but about holding the human source of the conscious energetic cording responsible for their choices to infiltrate you and attempts to influence your decision making and amplifying your emotions for their energetic benefit.

"IN THE NAME OF GOD"...

"I call for full retribution and justice"...

This is calling for payment from the human energetic cording for their interference. If you are in your heart, this decree is an appeal to God not to punish them but to stop them and hold them accountable for their deliberate energetic acts towards you. How they are held accountable is between them and God. If it is a concern of yours, then you are coming out of your heart and feeding your Ego. If things do not change after calling for retribution and justice, then this may be a karmic debt issue and may require communicating with your Higher Self for further guidance.

"for all cleared sources of <u>the word God</u>"…This is referencing all sources of energetic cording that were detached.

"in all directions of time, parallel universes and dimensions"…

"with unconditional love and forgiveness."….

"(1 x or optional)"…One appeal to God is all that is needed unless guided otherwise. This decree is optional.

THE CALLS TO GOD DECREES PROCEDURE

This procedure is for those who need a guideline to follow:

- **Center yourself** – Shut your eyes and imagine you have invisible arms on both sides of your body reaching as widely as possible. Then imagine these arms slowly pulling energy into your heart. Take a deep breath and slowly exhale. Open your eyes or keep them shut.
- **Move into your heart** – Imagine a ball of white fire about 3" above your crown chakra. Perceive it moving slowly, clockwise and downward towards your heart in alignment with your spine. Once the white ball of fire moves into your heart, wait until you perceive a "click" and hold it in place.
- **Say aloud or eternally**
  "In the Name of God, clear <u>the word God</u> from me in all directions of time, parallel universes and dimensions with unconditional love and forgiveness." (1x)

After you say the decree, perceive the effects. This may include waves of energy, feeling "snips and snaps" of cording detaching, or you may feel lighter.

DECREE FOR FULL RETRIBUTION AND JUSTICE (OPTIONAL)

"In the Name of God, I call for full retribution and justice for all cleared sources of <u>the word God</u> from me in all directions of time, parallel universes and dimensions with unconditional love and forgiveness." (1x & optional)

After you say the decree, perceive the effects. You may detect an overall feeling of peace and harmony.

The Clearing Decrees

1. Clearing Yourself
"In the Name of God, clear <u>me</u> in all directions of time, parallel universes and dimensions with unconditional love and forgiveness." *(1x)*

This basic decree can be utilized when you have negative thoughts about someone, something, or a particular situation that is repetitious or may come out of nowhere. It can be used when your mood swings from being positive to more negative without any direct cause. This is an indication of an energetic infiltration trying to manipulate your emotions to draw energy from you. Pay attention to when this happens and how often. You may choose to clear yourself first and then immediately attempt to clear the particular person or issue second to detach the energetic infiltration. Remember, this decree and sequence may have to be repeated many times depending upon if your frequency rate of vibration level is equal to or higher than the energetic infiltration energy.

2. Your Ego
"In the Name of God, clear <u>my ego</u> from me in all directions of time, parallel universes and dimensions with unconditional love and forgiveness." *(1x)*

The routine use of this decree is important. Earlier, it was discussed how your Ego may choose to impersonate your Higher Self in an attempt to keep you from reunification with God. When clearing yourself, consider clearing your Ego immediately after.

3. Chakras
"In the Name of God, clear my _____ chakra(s) from me (crown, third eye, throat, heart, solar plexus, sacral, root, etc.) in all directions of time, parallel universes and dimensions with unconditional love and forgiveness." (1x)

Special attention should be given to the sacral chakra. It is directly connected to your sexuality. When you are sexually intimate with another, you open your energy fields up to them. That leaves you vulnerable to their conscious energetic cording. *Sexual energy is the most powerful and sought after energy source in your body by conscious human energetic infiltrations.* It's important to clear your sacral chakra after every sexual encounter no matter who it may be. If not, you may find yourself energetically influenced by of all your sexual partners, past and present. If you are concerned about your choice of sexual partners, clear your sacral chakra of your sexual history and conscious human energetic cording:

Clearing Prior and Present Sexual Partners
"In the Name of God, clear _____ (sexual partner's name) from my sacral chakra in all directions of time, parallel universes and dimensions with unconditional love and forgiveness." (1x)

This, also, includes your present spouse or life partner. Though you may be in a committed relationship, it's important to clear yourself from your sexual partner and his/her sexual history. When sexually intimate, you are susceptible to energetic infiltration from your partner's past sexual liaisons through your sacral chakra.

#4. Body Systems
"In the Name of God, clear my _____ system (circulatory, endocrine, digestive, reproductive, muscle, bone, respiratory, lymphatic, etc.) in all directions of time, parallel universes and dimensions with unconditional love and forgiveness." (1x)

Those consciously walking their ascension path understand that there is a direct line that can be drawn between disease and energetics. This means that disease is considered a symptom of what is energetically out of balance within you. This can be due to exposure to specific environmental issues (EMF frequencies & causes), karmic debt, contracted life challenges, generational curses, etc. Conscious human energetic cording are also possible causes or if not the cause, they may connect to and amplify the symptom(s) to create a fear reaction in you. This is to receive a desired amount of energy without your consent and without detection.

#5. <u>Minor Miscellaneous Health Issues</u>
"In the Name of God, clear the source of my _____ (cough, sneezes, headache, fever, sore throat, aches & pains, etc.) from me in all directions of time, parallel universes and dimensions with unconditional love and forgiveness." (1x)

In the beginning, center your attention on the overall healing and then focus on the more specific symptoms. For example, you may have a metabolism health issue. Use the decree to detach the cords from the endocrine system first and then go back and clear your thyroid.

#6. <u>Traumas and Wounding</u>
"In the name of God, clear the sources of my _____ (sexual, physical, emotional, psychological, being a victim, being a bully, etc.) traumas and wounding from me in all directions of time, parallel universes and dimensions with unconditional love and forgiveness." (1x)

This is a blanket decree. It is meant to clear out the overall surface cording and their conscious human sources first. Then you go back and focus on clearing cording from more specific symptoms, underlying issues, the specific individuals involved and the fear attached the memories. Remember, conscious human energetic cording will amplify an emotion, especially if it is connected to some level of fear, to draw energy from you without detection.

#7. Addictions
"In the Name of God, clear the sources of my addiction to _____ (drugs, alcohol, cigarettes, shopping, sex, food, exercise, etc.) from me in all directions of time, parallel universes and dimensions with unconditional love and forgiveness." (1x)

This is a blanket decree. It will create a general, overall healing. When done, go back and focus on the more specific issues. For example, you may have a drug issue. Use the decree to detach the cords from "drugs" first and then go back and clear, for example, "prescription drugs" and then "oxycontin." Addictions are used by conscious human energetic cording to distract you from traveling your ascension path.

#8. Repetitious Thoughts
"In the Name of God, clear the source of my repetitive thoughts about _____ (person, situation, fear, etc.) from me in all directions of time, parallel universes and dimensions with unconditional love and forgiveness." (1x)

#9. Temper
"In the Name of God, clear the source of losing my temper _____ (with my child, at misplacing my car keys, getting up late for work, etc.) from me in all directions of time, parallel universes and dimensions with unconditional love and forgiveness." (1x)

#10. Media
"In the name of God, clear from me all media and their sources in all directions of time, parallel universes and dimensions with unconditional love and forgiveness." (1x)

Media today is a source of negative energy. It's time to take into consideration the amount of influence it has on all of us and who benefits. Living in a vacuum is not an answer but being very selective about what you expose yourself and family to energetically is important. Teaching yourself to use this decree when watching television, listening to music, etc. will help to detach any cording you or your family may have acquired while interacting with various forms of media.

#11. <u>Specific Media Clearings</u>
"In the Name of God, clear all _____ (websites, channelings, healer manuals, emails, books, articles, blogging sites, movies, CDs, DVDs, radio shows, music, etc.) and their sources from me in all directions of time, parallel universes and dimensions with unconditional love and forgiveness." (1x)

Words are very powerful. It does not matter if they are verbal or written. Clearing yourself of specific types of media is your personal responsibility that directly affects your spiritual and energetic health.

#12. <u>Healers, Clients, and Others</u>
"In the Name of God, clear _____ (person's name, name of healing system, organization, etc.) from me in all directions of time, parallel universes and dimensions with unconditional love and forgiveness." (1x)

This decree is also intended to be used if specific names of individuals need to be cleared.

When you give healings, you open up your energy fields or aura to your client. This allows conscious and unconscious human energetic cording. This is why some clients stay on your mind and they think about you. To prevent this and to work with integrity, clear yourself before the healing session, and clear again at the end. If guided to do so, clear cording during the session. This could be in conjunction with what you already do. As a client, you have a responsibility to do the same. This includes medical and dental appointments, body piercings, tattoos, manicures, pedicures, getting your hair cut, etc.

Remember to clear all healing systems you have been associated with as a healing practitioner, student or teacher, especially, if you received activations, healer lineages, and practiced any channeled procedures or healings. That includes the healing organizations and their leaders you are currently working with.

CHAPTER VIII.
A Sample Holistic Program

"If I have the belief that I can do it, I shall surely acquire the capacity to do it even if I may not have it at the beginning." MAHATMA GANDHI

FOR A PROGRAM OF this nature to work, the skills should be incorporated over a period of time and not all in one day. While doing this, you will still have to balance your life, face controversies and conflicts, and move through contracted life challenges. When you start routinely clearing yourself, these may become amplified as the old energies begin to surface and dissipate.

Below, I created a beginning level program to holistically incorporate the Calls to God decrees, symptoms of energetic infiltration, raising your frequency rate of vibration, and the energetic treatment of physical and mental conditions. I perceived that soul retrievals and choosing what wounding or traumas to clear should come from your spiritual guidance. This program is simple and makes it easy for you to document the addition of each decree and lifestyle change. It is imperative to be inside your heart and work with your inner guidance on doing this.

In the beginning, the most important Calls to God decrees to use routinely are *Clearing Yourself* and *Your Ego.* You may want to consider starting out just applying these two decrees the first week and using them as much as possible each day until they become a part of your everyday life. The empty bullets are spaces for you to document other decrees you chose to use. After you have become comfortable, ask your

Guidance to help you choose and incorporate more decrees that are in alignment with your ascension path.

The *Symptoms of Energetic Infiltration* is for you to keep track of those symptoms you are exhibiting. Then go to the Calls to God decrees manual and choose the clearing decrees that best match the symptoms. Repeat the decrees as often as you are guided to do so.

Week _____ to _____

Calls to God decrees

- #1. Clearing Yourself

- #2. My Ego

-

-

-

-

-

-

Symptoms of Energetic Infiltration

1. Swearing more than usual _____
2. Envy _____
3. Jealousy _____
4. Victimization _____
5. Physical Expression of anger _____
6. Repetitious thoughts about a person or situation _____
7. Blaming others for your situation or actions _____
8. Manipulating situations or others _____
9. Passing judgment _____
10. Cannot forgive yourself or others _____
11. Losing your temper _____
12. Overly concerned with abundance issues _____
13. Low self-esteem _____
14. Gossiping _____

This section on *How to Raise your Frequency Rate of Vibration* was included for you to document your progress at including energy enhancing lifestyle choices. As you can see, this is not a program you do for several months and stop. It is a *lifestyle change* to maintain and sustain your frequency rate of vibration to keep your spiritual defenses healthy and strong. As you choose a new energetic lifestyle choice, take as much time necessary to completely assimilate each one. This part is cumulative or you gradually add all the energetic lifestyle choices until you are practicing all of them at one time.

HOW TO RAISE YOUR FREQUENCY AND VIBRATION RATE?

Your Home
- Empty kitchen garbage daily _____
- Empty bathroom refuse daily _____
- Wash clothes often (undergarments) _____
- Use shower gel rather than bar soap _____

CLEANING YOUR HOME
- Use cleaners consisting of natural ingredients & high grade essential oils _____
- Clear food pantry regularly for expired food _____
- Clear and clean refrigerators for spoiled or old food _____
- Use high grade essential oil air diffusers _____
- Donate your unused or discarded clothes, after clearing them energetically _____

MEDITATION
- I meditate _____

PURIFY YOUR LIFESTYLE
- Stop tobacco use _____
- Stop alcohol consumption _____
- Eating more live foods than processed _____
- Modified meat consumption _____

DRINK
- Consuming fluids in their natural state _____
- Drinking warm or hot water with lemon _____

IMPECCABILITY

- Speaking from within my heart (neutrality, without judgment) _____

- Living in my heart (moving into my heart and not detaching in times of crisis) _____

ABUNDANCE

- Buying what I need and sometimes what I want _____

COMPASSION FOR OTHERS

This is something personal to be addressed between you and your Guidance.

This last part, *Energetically Treating Health Related Issues*, is very important. This is where we learn to practice the marriage of science and spirituality in our everyday lives and to embrace the tremendous positive impact it will have on your physical and mental wellbeing. Remember, this is not to take the place of the diagnosis and/or treatment of a certified, medically trained practitioners but to work congruently with them.

ENERGETICALLY TREATING HEALTH RELATED ISSUES

- Using decrees for minor first aid treatments
- Using decrees for symptoms of common communicable diseases _____ (fever, sinuses, chest congestion, coughs, sneezes, etc.)
- Using decrees for minor mental health issues _____ (sadness, outbursts of anger, symptoms of stress, etc.)

The main benefit from routinely clearing yourself and following your own holistic energetic healing program is a heightened perception to energy. You will become more sensitive to the media you expose yourself to, people you socialize with, the food you eat, the music you listen to, etc. In turn, you will have more control over the quality of your life.

AFTERWORD

As I had mentioned before, this book is a collaborative effort between God and me. It is my hope that my shared experiences with conscious human energetic infiltrations and their cording will inspire you to embrace your own spiritual freedom and relationship with God. You are not a leaf in the wind. You do not have to be energetically subjugated to others. De-cording will free you from the negative interference of others, will heighten your sensitivity to energy and will raise your frequency rate of vibration. Your quality of life will change for the better because you will be able to live in your heart. The energetic interferences will not have the influence that they had on you before you began de-cording. As I said before, you will still have your life challenges and karmic entanglements but *you will view them and act* from the perspective of a spiritual person having a human experience instead of a victim mired in chaos and conflict.

There is one more thing I would like to encourage you to do. I would like you to use the decrees below to check and clear my name and book for conscious human energetic cording. I feel I am to be held culpable to the same energetic standards as everyone else who publishes and presents information that has Divine input.

CALLS TO GOD DECREE #12. HEALERS, CLIENTS, AND OTHERS

"In the Name of God, clear *Susan K. Todd* from me in all directions of time, parallel universes and dimensions with unconditional love and forgiveness." (1x or as guided)

CALLS TO GOD DECREE #11. SPECIFIC MEDIA CLEARINGS

"In the Name of God, clear the book *Calls to God* by Susan K. Todd from me in all directions of time, parallel universes and dimensions with unconditional love and forgiveness." (1x or as guided)

GLOSSARY

<u>Conscious human energetic cording</u> – deliberately cording to another human for energy takings and manipulation without the other's consent

<u>Cording</u> – etheric, energetic conduits or tubing

<u>De-cording</u> – cutting and clearing unwanted energetic cording from a human source

<u>Energetic infiltrations</u> – subtle energy ties or cording sent from one human source to another

<u>Holistic</u> – focus is on the balance of all parts not just one

<u>Human energetic cording</u> – etheric, energetic conduits or tubing that originates from a human source

<u>Implied consent</u> – in the energetic world, if you do not routinely clear yourself of cording then it is interpreted that the human sources of these energetic cording can take all the energy they want from you

<u>Living in your heart</u> – your contact with God, place of complete neutrality

<u>Soul fragmentation</u> – when parts of your soul fragments or leaves you during times of deep trauma and wounding

<u>Soul retrieval</u> – act of your soul fragments coming back to make your soul whole again

<u>Spiritual circuitry</u> – psychic abilities, telepathic abilities, intuition, consciousness, energetic awareness and sensitivity

<u>Unconscious human energetic cording</u> – cording between humans without either of them being aware